PURSUE

J O U R N A L

PONCHO LOWDER

@PASTORPONCHO

Regal

From Gospel Light
Ventura, California, U.S.A.

Published by Regal
From Gospel Light
Ventura, California, U.S.A.
www.regalbooks.com
Printed in the U.S.A.

Edited by Leslie MacGregor

Rights for publishing this book outside the U.S.A. or in non-English languages are
administered by Gospel Light Worldwide, an international not-for-profit ministry.
For additional information, please visit www.glww.org, email info@glww.org, or write to
Gospel Light Worldwide, 1957 Eastman Avenue, Ventura, CA 93003, U.S.A.

To order copies of this book and other Regal products in bulk quantities,
please contact us at 1-800-446-7735.

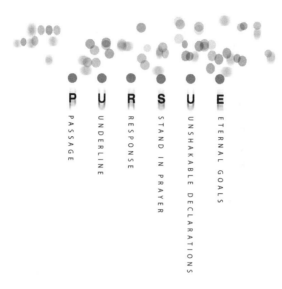

P   **U**   **R**   **S**   **U**   **E**

PASSAGE   UNDERLINE   RESPONSE   STAND IN PRAYER   UNSHAKABLE DECLARATIONS   ETERNAL GOALS

Follow us on Twitter
Go to www.Twitter.com/PursueGod

Check us out online at www.PursueGod.com

Add us on Facebook
Go to www.Facebook.com/PursueGod

Download the PursueGod mobile app from
www.PursueGod.com

Free Music Download

Get 2 free song downloads from Generation Unleashed. Your devotional time will be better then ever as you listen to 8,000 young people worship Jesus with one voice. Recorded live at the Generation Unleashed Conference in Portland Oregon. Download the entire digital album for $7.99.

✳ I Am Alive

✳ He Lives

To download free songs go to
www.PursueGod.com
Click on "Music" tab

PursueGod Mobile App

Download the app today at
www.PursueGod.com

About the PURSUE Journal

The PURSUE Journal is designed to be a tool to help you PURSUE God in your daily devotions. It is meant to become you and your Bible's best friend. As you use the PURSUE Journal, you will find there is a consistent pattern, guide and accountability that will help you develop a deeper relationship with Jesus as you PURSUE Him daily.

 NAME

 EMAIL

JOURNAL START DATE

JOURNAL END DATE

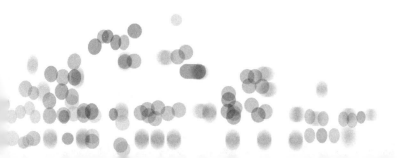

Journal Resources

Bible Reading Plan

By using the Bible reading plan on pages 12-15, you will be daily built up with wisdom and faith for the journey in front of you. The Bible reading plan will walk you each year through the Old Testament once, the New Testament twice, and Proverbs twice. It is laid out in such a way that you will be in passages from the Old and New Testaments almost every day.

Prayer Section

Don't allow the quality of your prayer life to be dictated by your daily emotional state of being! The prayer section on pages 16-19 will help guide you through your prayer time. As you take time daily to stand in prayer, you will find it to be helpful to have a list all the people, items and goals you have. There are also Scriptures and prayer request pages for writing out your prayer requests and for looking back as God answers your prayers.

Unshakable Declarations

Take time to memorize the 10 unshakable declarations on pages 20-21 and the verses that go with them. Know what the Bible says about you and declare it over your life!

Scriptures to Memorize

Take time to hide God's Word in your heart. As you spend time each day in devotions, look for passages that really speak to you and memorize them (see page 24). If you memorize just one passage a week, in one year you will have more than 50 powerful Scriptures locked into memory. This will help you to share your faith, pray with power, and stand against the temptations of this world.

● Response Journal Pages

The Response pages are designed to be used daily for you to write out what God has spoken to you through His Word. As you write your responses, focus on the passages you underlined during your Bible reading time. Afterward, be sure to log it in your table of contents on pages 10 and 11.

● Recommended Materials (see page 159)

Flee the evil desires of youth, and pursue righteousness, faith, love and peace, along with those who call on the Lord out of a pure heart (2 Timothy 2:22, *NIV*).

PURSUE GOD
By Poncho Lowder

Pursue God is the ultimate companion to your *Pursue Journal*. In this book, Pastor Poncho teaches you how to fully use your *Pursue Journal* to maximize your devotions. With the fast pace of our culture today, people struggle more than ever with developing a daily relationship with God, and, often, those who do have a daily time with God may find themselves doing it out of duty rather than a personal relationship with Him. *Pursue God* helps readers develop an authentic daily relationship where they are inspired to pursue God—first, by discussing "why" to pursue God, and second, by showing "how" to effectively pursue Him.

ISBN: 978-0-8307-6180-7

Visit us at www.PursueGod.com

Daily Approach to Your PURSUE Devotional Time

Passage

Take time to read through the daily passages listed in the Bible reading plan on pages 12-15. Let the Word of God get into your heart and mind as you do your devotional reading.

> *My son, keep my words and store up my commands within you. Keep my commands and you will live; guard my teachings as the apple of your eye* (Proverbs 7:1-3, *NIV*).

Underline

Personalize your Bible as you read by underlining, circling and highlighting the items that really speak to you. Make sure to also underline places where you feel God is speaking to you.

> *For the word of God is living and active. Sharper than any double-edged sword, it penetrates even to dividing soul and spirit, joints and marrow; it judges the thoughts and attitudes of the heart* (Hebrews 4:12, *NIV*).

Response

Write out and respond to the things that God has spoken to you through His Word. Journal where you are at in life and what you feel God is calling you to do.

> *Then the LORD replied: "Write down the revelation and make it plain on tablets so that a herald may run with it"* (Habakkuk 2:2, *NIV*).

● **S**tand in Prayer

Pray and believe for great things in, around and through your life. Use the prayer section on pages 16 through 19 to guide you as you stand in prayer.

> *Call to me and I will answer you and tell you great and unsearchable things you do not know* (Jeremiah 33:3, *NIV*).

● **U**nshakable Declarations

During your time of prayer, declare the Word of God over your life. Refer to the declarations on pages 20 and 21, and add some of your own.

> *I will give you the keys of the kingdom of heaven; whatever you bind on earth will be bound in heaven, and whatever you loose on earth will be loosed in heaven* (Matthew 16:19, *NIV*).

● **E**ternal Goals

As you use the PURSUE Journal, you will find yourself growing deeper in your relationship with God. Take time daily to set goals that have eternal value. Look at some of these goals listed on page 21 and let them challenge you to each day to pursue God's will.

> *The Spirit of the Lord is on me, because he has anointed me to preach good news to the poor. He has sent me to proclaim freedom for the prisoners and recovery of sight for the blind, to release the oppressed, to proclaim the year of the Lord's favor* (Luke 4:18-19, *NIV*).

Table of Contents

These next two pages are designed so that you can personalize the Table of Contents of your PURSUE Journal as you fill out your Response journal pages. Simply put the date, passage and your personal title/topic for that day along with the page number with which it coincides.

Page	Date	Passage	Title/Topic

Page	Date	Passage	Title/Topic

Bible Reading Plan

January

- [ ] 1. Prov. 1; John 1–2
- [ ] 2. Ps. 1; John 3–5
- [ ] 3. Prov. 2; John 6–7
- [ ] 4. Ps. 2; John 8–10
- [ ] 5. Prov. 3; John 11–12
- [ ] 6. Ps. 3; John 13–15
- [ ] 7. Ps. 4; John 16–19
- [ ] 8. Prov. 4–5; John 20–21
- [ ] 9. Luke 1–4
- [ ] 10. Ps. 5; Luke 5–7
- [ ] 11. Prov. 6; Luke 8–9
- [ ] 12. Ps. 6; Luke 10–12
- [ ] 13. Prov. 7; Luke 13–15
- [ ] 14. Ps. 7; Luke 16–18
- [ ] 15. Prov. 8; Luke 19–21
- [ ] 16. Luke 22–24
- [ ] 17. Acts 1–4
- [ ] 18. Pss. 8–9; Acts 5–7
- [ ] 19. Prov. 9–10; Acts 8–10
- [ ] 20. Ps. 10; Acts 11–13
- [ ] 21. Prov. 11; Acts 14–16
- [ ] 22. Ps. 11; Acts 17–20
- [ ] 23. Prov. 12; Acts 21–23
- [ ] 24. Ps. 12; Acts 24–27
- [ ] 25. Acts 28; Philippians
- [ ] 26. Ephesians
- [ ] 27. Prov. 13–14; Rom. 1–3
- [ ] 28. Pss. 13–15; Rom. 4–7
- [ ] 29. Prov. 15; Rom. 8–10
- [ ] 30. Rom. 11–16
- [ ] 31. Galatians

February

- [ ] 1. Ps. 16; 1 Cor. 1–6
- [ ] 2. Prov. 16; 1 Cor. 7–11
- [ ] 3. 1 Cor. 12–16
- [ ] 4. Ps. 17; 2 Cor. 1–6
- [ ] 5. Prov. 17; 2 Cor. 7–11
- [ ] 6. 2 Cor. 12–13; Colossians
- [ ] 7. Ps. 18; 1 Thess.
- [ ] 8. Prov. 18–19; 2 Thess.
- [ ] 9. Ps. 19; 1 Peter
- [ ] 10. Prov. 20; 2 Peter
- [ ] 11. Pss. 20–21; 1 Tim.
- [ ] 12. Prov. 21; 2 Tim.
- [ ] 13. Titus; Jude
- [ ] 14. Ps. 22; 1 John
- [ ] 15. Philemon; Heb. 1–4
- [ ] 16. Ps. 23; Heb. 5–9
- [ ] 17. Prov. 22; Heb. 10–13
- [ ] 18. Ps. 24; James
- [ ] 19. 2 John; 3 John; Matt. 1–2
- [ ] 20. Prov. 23; Matt. 3–5
- [ ] 21. Prov. 24; Matt. 6–8
- [ ] 22. Prov. 25; Matt. 9–11
- [ ] 23. Prov. 26; Matt. 12–13
- [ ] 24. Prov. 27; Matt. 14–17
- [ ] 25. Prov. 28; Matt. 18–20
- [ ] 26. Prov. 29; Matt. 21–23
- [ ] 27. Prov. 30; Matt. 24–25
- [ ] 28. Prov. 31; Matt. 26–28

March

- [ ] 1. Ps. 25; Mark 1–3
- [ ] 2. Ps. 26; Mark 4–6
- [ ] 3. Ps. 27; Mark 7–9
- [ ] 4. Ps. 28; Mark 10–12
- [ ] 5. Ps. 29; Mark 13–14
- [ ] 6. Pss. 30–31; Mark 15–16
- [ ] 7. Rev. 1–5
- [ ] 8. Ps. 32; Rev. 6–10
- [ ] 9. Ps. 33; Rev. 11–15
- [ ] 10. Ps. 34; Rev. 16–19
- [ ] 11. Ps. 35; Rev. 20–22
- [ ] 12. Ps. 36; Gen. 1–3
- [ ] 13. Ps. 37; Gen. 4–7
- [ ] 14. Ps. 38; Gen. 8–10
- [ ] 15. Ps. 39; Gen. 11–15
- [ ] 16. Ps. 40; Gen. 16–19
- [ ] 17. Ps. 41; Gen. 20–23
- [ ] 18. Ps. 42; Gen. 24–25
- [ ] 19. Ps. 43; Gen. 26–28
- [ ] 20. Ps. 44; Gen. 29–30
- [ ] 21. Ps. 45; Gen. 31–32
- [ ] 22. Ps. 46; Gen. 33–36
- [ ] 23. Ps. 47; Gen. 37–40
- [ ] 24. Ps. 48; Gen. 41–43
- [ ] 25. Ps. 49; Gen. 44–46
- [ ] 26. Ps. 50; Gen. 47–50
- [ ] 27. Ps. 51; Exod. 1–4
- [ ] 28. Ps. 52; Exod. 5–8
- [ ] 29. Ps. 53; Exod. 9–12
- [ ] 30. Ps. 54; Exod. 13–16
- [ ] 31. Ps. 55; Exod. 17–20

Get daily updates at www.PursueGod.com & Facebook.com/PursueGod
or get daily text reminders at twitter.com/PursueGod

Bible Reading Plan

April

- ☐ 1. Ps. 56; Exod. 21–23
- ☐ 2. Ps. 57; Exod. 24–28
- ☐ 3. Ps. 58; Exod. 29–31
- ☐ 4. Ps. 59; Exod. 32–34
- ☐ 5. Ps. 60; Exod. 35–37
- ☐ 6. Ps. 61; Exod. 38–40
- ☐ 7. Ps. 62; Lev. 1–5
- ☐ 8. Ps. 63; Lev. 6–8
- ☐ 9. Ps. 64; Lev 9–12
- ☐ 10. Ps. 65; Lev. 13–14
- ☐ 11. Ps. 66; Lev. 15–18
- ☐ 12. Ps. 67; Lev. 19–22
- ☐ 13. Ps. 68; Lev. 23–25
- ☐ 14. Ps. 69; Lev. 26–27
- ☐ 15. Ps. 70; Num. 1–3
- ☐ 16. Ps. 71; Num. 4–6
- ☐ 17. Ps. 72; Num. 7–8
- ☐ 18. Ps. 73; Num. 9–11
- ☐ 19. Ps. 74; Num. 12–14
- ☐ 20. Ps. 75; Num. 15–17
- ☐ 21. Ps. 76; Num. 18–20
- ☐ 22. Ps. 77; Num. 21–22
- ☐ 23. Ps. 78; Num. 23–24
- ☐ 24. Ps. 79; Num. 25–27
- ☐ 25. Ps. 80; Num. 28–30
- ☐ 26. Ps. 81; Num. 31–33
- ☐ 27. Ps. 82; Num. 34–36
- ☐ 28. Ps. 83; Deut. 1–3
- ☐ 29. Ps. 84; Deut. 4–6
- ☐ 30. Ps. 85; Deut. 7–10

May

- ☐ 1. Ps. 86; Deut. 11–14
- ☐ 2. Ps. 87; Deut. 15–19
- ☐ 3. Ps. 88; Deut. 20–23
- ☐ 4. Ps. 89; Deut. 24–27
- ☐ 5. Ps. 90; Deut. 28–29
- ☐ 6. Ps. 91; Deut. 30–32
- ☐ 7. Ps. 92; Deut. 33–34
- ☐ 8. Ps. 93; Josh. 1–5
- ☐ 9. Ps. 94; Josh. 6–8
- ☐ 10. Ps. 95; Josh. 9–11
- ☐ 11. Ps. 96; Josh. 12–15
- ☐ 12. Ps. 97; Josh. 16–19
- ☐ 13. Josh. 20–24
- ☐ 14. Pss. 98–99; Judg. 1–3
- ☐ 15. Ps. 100; Judg. 4–6
- ☐ 16. Ps. 101; Judg. 7–9
- ☐ 17. Ps. 102; Judg. 10–13
- ☐ 18. Ps. 103; Judg. 14–16
- ☐ 19. Ps. 104; Judg. 17–19
- ☐ 20. Ps. 105; Judg. 20–21
- ☐ 21. Ps. 106; Ruth
- ☐ 22. Ps. 107; 1 Sam. 1–2
- ☐ 23. Ps. 108; 1 Sam. 3–7
- ☐ 24. Ps. 109; 1 Sam 8–11
- ☐ 25. Ps. 110; 1 Sam. 12–14
- ☐ 26. Ps. 111; 1 Sam. 15–17
- ☐ 27. Ps. 112; 1 Sam. 18–21
- ☐ 28. Ps. 113; 1 Sam. 22–25
- ☐ 29. Ps. 114; 1 Sam. 26–31
- ☐ 30. Ps. 115; 2 Sam. 1–3
- ☐ 31. Ps. 116; 2 Sam. 4–8

June

- ☐ 1. Ps. 117; 2 Sam. 9–12
- ☐ 2. Ps. 118; 2 Sam. 13–15
- ☐ 3. Ps. 119
- ☐ 4. Ps. 120; 2 Sam. 16–18
- ☐ 5. Ps. 121; 2 Sam. 19–21
- ☐ 6. Ps. 122; 2 Sam. 22–24
- ☐ 7. Ps. 123; 1 Kings 1–3
- ☐ 8. Ps. 124; 1 Kings 4–6
- ☐ 9. Ps. 125; 1 Kings 7–8
- ☐ 10. Ps. 126; 1 Kings 9–11
- ☐ 11. Ps. 127; 1 Kings 12–14
- ☐ 12. Ps. 128; 1 Kings 15–17
- ☐ 13. Ps. 129; 1 Kings 18–20
- ☐ 14. Ps. 130; 1 Kings 21–22
- ☐ 15. Ps. 131; 2 Kings 1–4
- ☐ 16. Ps. 132; 2 Kings 5–7
- ☐ 17. Ps. 133; 2 Kings 8–10
- ☐ 18. Ps. 134; 2 Kings 11–14
- ☐ 19. Ps. 135; 2 Kings 15–17
- ☐ 20. Ps. 136; 2 Kings 18–20
- ☐ 21. Ps. 137; 2 Kings 21–23
- ☐ 22. Ps. 138; 2 Kings 24–25
- ☐ 23. Ps. 139; 1 Chron. 1–2
- ☐ 24. Ps. 140; 1 Chron. 3–5
- ☐ 25. Ps. 141; 1 Chron. 6–7
- ☐ 26. Ps. 142; 1 Chron. 8–11
- ☐ 27. Ps. 143; 1 Chron. 12–15
- ☐ 28. Ps. 144; 1 Chron. 16–19
- ☐ 29. Ps. 145; 1 Chron. 20–23
- ☐ 30. Ps. 146; 1 Chron. 24–27

Get daily updates at www.PursueGod.com & Facebook.com/PursueGod
or get daily text reminders at twitter.com/PursueGod

Bible Reading Plan

July

- [ ] 1. Ps. 147; 1 Chron. 28–29
- [ ] 2. Ps. 148; 2 Chron. 1–5
- [ ] 3. Pss. 149–150; 2 Chron. 6–8
- [ ] 4. Matt. 1; 2 Chron. 9–11
- [ ] 5. Matt. 2; 2 Chron. 12 –16
- [ ] 6. Matt. 3; 2 Chron. 17–20
- [ ] 7. Matt. 4; 2 Chron. 21–24
- [ ] 8. Matt. 5; 2 Chron. 25–26
- [ ] 9. Matt. 6; 2 Chron. 27–29
- [ ] 10. Matt. 7; 2 Chron. 30–32
- [ ] 11. Matt. 8; 2 Chron. 33–34
- [ ] 12. Matt. 9; 2 Chron. 35–36
- [ ] 13. Matt. 10; Ezra 1–4
- [ ] 14. Matt. 11; Ezra 5–8
- [ ] 15. Matt. 12; Ezra 9–10
- [ ] 16. Matt. 13; Neh. 1–3
- [ ] 17. Matt. 14; Neh. 4–7
- [ ] 18. Matt. 15; Neh. 8–9
- [ ] 19. Matt. 16; Neh. 10–11
- [ ] 20. Matt. 17; Neh. 12–13
- [ ] 21. Matt. 18; Esther 1–4
- [ ] 22. Matt. 19; Esther 5–10
- [ ] 23. Matt. 20; Job 1–4
- [ ] 24. Matt. 21; Job 5–7
- [ ] 25. Matt. 22; Job 8–11
- [ ] 26. Matt. 23; Job 12–15
- [ ] 27. Matt. 24; Job 16–19
- [ ] 28. Matt. 25; Job 20–22
- [ ] 29. Matt. 26; Job 23–25
- [ ] 30. Matt. 27; Job 26–29
- [ ] 31. Matt. 28; Job 30–32

August

- [ ] 1. Mark 1; Job 33–34
- [ ] 2. Mark 2; Job 35–38
- [ ] 3. Mark 3; Job 39–42
- [ ] 4. Mark 4; Eccles. 1–3
- [ ] 5. Mark 5; Eccles. 4–7
- [ ] 6. Mark 6; Eccles. 8–10
- [ ] 7. Mark 7; Eccles. 11–12
- [ ] 8. Mark 8; Song of Sol. 1–4
- [ ] 9. Mark 9; Song of Sol. 5–8
- [ ] 10. Mark 10; Isa. 1–2
- [ ] 11. Mark 11; Isa. 3–5
- [ ] 12. Mark 12; Isa 6–8
- [ ] 13. Mark 13; Isa. 9–10
- [ ] 14. Mark 14; Isa. 11–12
- [ ] 15. Mark 15; Isa. 13–14
- [ ] 16. Mark 16; Isa. 15–19
- [ ] 17. Luke 1; Isa. 20–21
- [ ] 18. Luke 2; Isa. 22–23
- [ ] 19. Luke 3; Isa. 24–26
- [ ] 20. Luke 4; Isa 27–28
- [ ] 21. Luke 5; Isa. 29–30
- [ ] 22. Luke 6; Isa. 31–33
- [ ] 23. Luke 7; Isa. 34–36
- [ ] 24. Luke 8; Isa. 37
- [ ] 25. Luke 9; Isa. 38–39
- [ ] 26. Luke 10; Isa. 40–41
- [ ] 27. Luke 11; Isa. 42–43
- [ ] 28. Luke 12; Isa. 44–45
- [ ] 29. Luke 13; Isa. 46–48
- [ ] 30. Luke 14; Isa 49–51
- [ ] 31. Luke 15; Isa 52–55

September

- [ ] 1. Luke 16; Isa. 56–58
- [ ] 2. Luke 17; Isa. 59–61
- [ ] 3. Luke 18; Isa. 62–64
- [ ] 4. Luke 19; Isa. 65–66
- [ ] 5. Luke 20; Jer. 1–2
- [ ] 6. Luke 21; Jer. 3–4
- [ ] 7. Luke 22; Jer. 5
- [ ] 8. Luke 23; Jer. 6–7
- [ ] 9. Luke 24; Jer. 8–9
- [ ] 10. John 1; Jer. 10–11
- [ ] 11. John 2; Jer. 12–14
- [ ] 12. John 3; Jer. 15–17
- [ ] 13. John 4; Jer. 18–20
- [ ] 14. John 5; Jer. 21–22
- [ ] 15. John 6; Jer. 23–24
- [ ] 16. John 7; Jer. 25–27
- [ ] 17. John 8; Jer. 28–29
- [ ] 18. John 9; Jer. 30–31
- [ ] 19. John 10; Jer. 32–33
- [ ] 20. John 11; Jer. 34–36
- [ ] 21. John 12; Jer. 37–39
- [ ] 22. John 13; Jer. 40–43
- [ ] 23. John 14; Jer. 44–46
- [ ] 24. John 15; Jer. 47– 48
- [ ] 25. John 16; Jer. 49
- [ ] 26. John 17; Jer. 50
- [ ] 27. John 18; Jer. 51
- [ ] 28. John 19; Jer. 52
- [ ] 29. John 20; Lam. 1–2
- [ ] 30. John 21; Lam. 3–5

Bible Reading Plan

October

- [ ] 1. Acts 1; Ezek. 1–3
- [ ] 2. Acts 2; Ezek. 4–6
- [ ] 3. Acts 3; Ezek. 7–9
- [ ] 4. Acts 4; Ezek. 10–11
- [ ] 5. Acts 5; Ezek. 12–13
- [ ] 6. Acts 6; Ezek. 14–16
- [ ] 7. Acts 7; Ezek. 17
- [ ] 8. Acts 8; Ezek. 18
- [ ] 9. Acts 9; Ezek. 19–20
- [ ] 10. Acts 10; Ezek. 21–22
- [ ] 11. Acts 11; Ezek. 23–24
- [ ] 12. Acts 12; Ezek. 25–26
- [ ] 13. Acts 13; Ezek. 27
- [ ] 14. Acts 14; Ezek. 28–29
- [ ] 15. Acts 15; Ezek. 30–31
- [ ] 16. Acts 16; Ezek. 32–33
- [ ] 17. Acts 17; Ezek. 34–36
- [ ] 18. Acts 18; Ezek. 37–39
- [ ] 19. Acts 19; Ezek. 40–43
- [ ] 20. Acts 20; Ezek. 44
- [ ] 21. Acts 21; Ezek. 45–46
- [ ] 22. Acts 22; Ezek. 47–48
- [ ] 23. Acts 23; Dan. 1–2
- [ ] 24. Acts 24; Dan. 3–4
- [ ] 25. Acts 25; Dan. 5–6
- [ ] 26. Acts 26; Dan. 7–8
- [ ] 27. Acts 27; Dan. 9–10
- [ ] 28. Acts 28; Dan. 11–12
- [ ] 29. Rom. 1–2; Hos. 1–2
- [ ] 30. Rom. 3–4; Hos. 3–4
- [ ] 31. Rom. 5–6; Hos. 5–6

November

- [ ] 1. Rom. 7–8; Hos. 7
- [ ] 2. Rom. 9–10; Hos. 8
- [ ] 3. Rom. 11–12; Hos. 9
- [ ] 4. Rom. 13–14; Hos. 10
- [ ] 5. Rom. 15–16; Hos. 11
- [ ] 6. 1 Cor. 1–2; Hos. 12–13
- [ ] 7. 1 Cor. 3–4; Hos. 14
- [ ] 8. 1 Cor. 5–6; Joel 1
- [ ] 9. 1 Cor. 7–8; Joel 2
- [ ] 10. 1 Cor. 9–10; Joel 3
- [ ] 11. 1 Cor. 11–12; Amos 1
- [ ] 12. 1 Cor. 13–14; Amos 2–3
- [ ] 13. 1 Cor. 15–16; Amos 4
- [ ] 14. 2 Cor. 1–2; Amos 5
- [ ] 15. 2 Cor. 3–5; Amos 6
- [ ] 16. 2 Cor. 6–8; Amos 7
- [ ] 17. 2 Cor. 9–11; Amos 8
- [ ] 18. 2 Cor. 12–13; Amos 9
- [ ] 19. Gal. 1–3; Obadiah
- [ ] 20. Gal. 4–6; Jonah 1
- [ ] 21. Eph. 1–3; Jonah 2
- [ ] 22. Eph. 4–6; Jonah 3
- [ ] 23. Phil. 1–2; Jonah 4
- [ ] 24. Phil. 3–4; Micah 1
- [ ] 25. Col. 1–2; Micah 2
- [ ] 26. Col. 3–4; Micah 3
- [ ] 27. 1 Thess. 1–2; Micah 4
- [ ] 28. 1 Thess. 3–5; Micah 5
- [ ] 29. 2 Thess. 1–3; Micah 6
- [ ] 30. 1 Tim. 1–3; Micah 7

December

- [ ] 1. 1 Tim. 4–6; Nah. 1
- [ ] 2. 2 Tim. 1–2; Nah. 2–3
- [ ] 3. 2 Tim. 3–4; Hab. 1–2
- [ ] 4. Titus 1–3; Hab. 3
- [ ] 5. Philemon; Zeph. 1–2
- [ ] 6. Heb. 1–2; Zeph. 3
- [ ] 7. Heb. 3–4; Hag. 1–2
- [ ] 8. Heb. 5–6; Zech. 1–2
- [ ] 9. Heb. 7–8; Zech. 3–4
- [ ] 10. Heb. 9–10; Zech. 5–6
- [ ] 11. Heb. 11; Zech. 7–8
- [ ] 12. Heb. 12–13; Zech. 9–10
- [ ] 13. Jas. 1–2; Zech. 11–12
- [ ] 14. Jas. 3–4; Zech. 13–14
- [ ] 15. Jas. 5; Mal. 1–3
- [ ] 16. 1 Pet. 1–2; Prov. 1–2
- [ ] 17. 1 Pet. 3–5; Prov. 3–4
- [ ] 18. 2 Pet. 1–3; Prov. 5–6
- [ ] 19. 1 John 1–2; Prov. 7–8
- [ ] 20. 1 John 3–5; Prov. 9–10
- [ ] 21. 2 John; 3 John; Prov. 11–12
- [ ] 22. Jude; Prov. 13–15
- [ ] 23. Rev. 1–2; Prov. 16–17
- [ ] 24. Rev. 3–5; Prov. 18–19
- [ ] 25. Rev. 6–7; Prov. 20–21
- [ ] 26. Rev. 8–10; Prov. 22–23
- [ ] 27. Rev. 11–12; Prov. 24–25
- [ ] 28. Rev. 13–14; Prov. 26–27
- [ ] 29. Rev. 15–17; Prov. 28–29
- [ ] 30. Rev. 18–19; Prov. 30
- [ ] 31. Rev. 20–22; Prov. 31

Get daily updates at www.PursueGod.com & Facebook.com/PursueGod
or get daily text reminders at twitter.com/PursueGod

About Prayer

Prayer Is Relating to God
In my prayer time today, I want to focus on developing
a deeper relationship with my Savior.

Prayer Takes Faith in God's Ability
In my prayer time today, I will stretch my faith and
believe for great things beyond my ability.

Prayer Requires Trust in God's Timing
Today I will put all my confidence in God
and His perfect timing for my life.

Prayer Involves Asking
Today I will ask according to God's will.

Prayer Is Motivated by Love
Today I will make sure all my prayers are motivated
by love for God.

Prayer Must Have Passion
I will be passionate in my prayer time today
as I seek God's will.

Prayer Brings Alignment
Today I will pray that God will show me any areas where
I need to align with His Word.

Prayer Is Purpose-Driven
Today I will pray for the purposes of God to be done
in and through my life.

Standing in Prayer for . . .

Colossians 4:2, NIV
Devote yourselves to prayer, being watchful and thankful.

✳ People

✳ Things

✳ Goals

www.PursueGod.com

Praying the Lord's Prayer

Matthew 6:9-13, NIV

Use this prayer to help direct you as you pray daily.
Remember: It's not ment to be recited, prayer is relational.

Our *Father* in heaven . . .

Father, I am Your child and I carry your Spirit, blessing and anointing. I am never alone, because You are my perfect Father who will truly love and care for me.

Hallowed be your *name* . . .

Lord, help me to glorify Your name and be consumed with the desire of knowing You.

Your kingdom come, *your will* be done on earth as it is in heaven . . .

Lord, help me to not be distracted today by my own desires, but whatever You, Father, want to do in and through me, let that be done. I surrender my will to You, Lord. Let Your will be done in my life today.

Give us *today* our daily bread . . .

Lord, I ask that You would give me something practical and real from Your Word that will challenge and strengthen me. Please provide for all my needs today, both spiritual and natural.

Forgive us our debts, *as we also have forgiven* our debtors . . .

Father, search me for anything that would separate me from You or cause you pain. Fill me with Your Spirit and grace so that I can forgive and love as You do.

And lead us not into *temptation*, but deliver us from the evil one

Father, prepare me to stand against anything today that would lead me away from Your presence, and keep me from temptation.

Prayer

Today I Am Believing for . . .

● **Matthew 21:22, NIV**

If you believe, you will receive whatever you ask for in prayer.

Write down what you are believing for . . .

_____

_____

_____

_____

_____

_____

_____

_____

_____

_____

_____

_____

_____

_____

_____

_____

_____

_____

_____

_____

● **Philippians 4:6-7, NIV**

Do not be anxious about anything, but in everything, by prayer and petition, with thanksgiving, present your requests to God. And the peace of God, which transcends all understanding, will guard your hearts and your minds in Christ Jesus.

Prayer

// 19 //

Unshakable Declarations

Hebrews 12:28-29, NIV

Therefore, since we are receiving a kingdom that cannot be shaken, let us be thankful, and so worship God acceptably with reverence and awe, for our "God is a consuming fire."

✳ I Am a New Creation in Christ!

Therefore, if anyone is in Christ, he is a new creation; the old has gone, the new has come! (2 Corinthians 5:17, NIV).

✳ I Am Called to Preach the Gospel!

Go into all the world and preach the Good News to everyone, everywhere (Mark 16:15, NLT).

✳ I Have a Great Future!

"For I know the plans I have for you," declares the LORD, "plans to prosper you and not to harm you, plans to give you hope and a future" (Jeremiah 29:11, NIV).

✳ I Can Do All Things Through Christ!

I can do all things through Christ who strengthens me (Philippians 4:13, NKJV).

✳ By His Stripes I Am Healed!

But he was wounded and crushed for our sins. He was beaten that we might have peace. He was whipped, and we were healed! (Isaiah 53:5, NLT).

✳ No Weapon Formed Against Me Shall Prosper!

No weapon that is formed against you will prosper (Isaiah 54:17, NASB).

✳ I Will Not Give in to Temptation!

But remember that the temptations that come into your life are no different from what others experience. And God is faithful. He will keep the temptation from becoming so strong that you can't stand up against it. When you are tempted, he will show you a way out so that you will not give in to it (1 Corinthians 10:13, NLT).

www.PursueGod.com

✳ God Will Speak to Me Today as I Pray!
Call to me and I will answer you and tell you great and unsearchable things you do not know (Jeremiah 33:3, *NIV*).

✳ I Am Free in Christ!
It is for freedom that Christ has set us free. Stand firm, then, and do not let yourselves be burdened again by a yoke of slavery (Galatians 5:1, *NIV*).

✳ I Am Pure in Christ!
If we confess our sins, he is faithful and just and will forgive us our sins and purify us from all unrighteousness (1 John 1:9, *NIV*).

Eternal Goals

- ● I will share my faith with someone today.
- ● I will meet someone's need today.
- ● I will build others up today with my words.
- ● I will draw near to God throughout my day.
- ● I will live life on purpose today.

Preaching the Gospel Message

● Mark 16:15, NLT

Go into all the world and preach the Good News to everyone, everywhere.

Statistics show us that 95 percent of all Christians have never led anyone to Christ. Many young people are full of fear and doubt about their ability to share the gospel. If this is true of your life, you need to stir your faith daily to share the gospel message with the people whom God brings into your path. Just like anything else, evangelism requires effort and practice.

Below are four simple truths for you to memorize that will help you share your faith as God opens the doors. Remember that people don't understand that they need to be saved unless they first understand they are lost. Let these four truths help guide you as you share the gospel message.

1. **GOD:** God created us so He could have a relationship with us.

   In the Garden of Eden, He would spend time with Adam and Eve. They were the only beings in His creation that were created in His image.

   So God created man in his own image, in the image of God he created him; male and female he created them. God blessed them and said to them, "Be fruitful and increase in number; fill the earth and subdue it. Rule over the fish of the sea and the birds of the air and over every living creature that moves on the ground" (Genesis 1:27-28, NIV).

2. **MAN:** God gave man the ability to choose what he wanted to do.

   God gave us the ability to choose how we are going to live. The price of true love means that people can choose to love you or hate you . . .

Unshakabele Declarations

For all have sinned and fall short of the glory of God (Romans 3:23, *NIV*).

3. **PROBLEM:** Man sinned, and it separated him from God. Sin has consequences.

   Sin is what separates us from God. All of us are sinners, and because of our own actions, we all condemn ourselves to hell.

   For the wages of sin is death, but the gift of God is eternal life in Christ Jesus our Lord (Romans 6:23, *NIV*).

4. **SOLUTION:** Jesus gave His life to pay for our sins. This made a way for us to go to heaven.

   We can't fix our sin problem on our own. The only way for us to be forgiven is to ask Jesus to forgive us. He lived a perfect life and gave His life on the cross so we could be forgiven of our sins.

   If you confess with your mouth, "Jesus is Lord," and believe in your heart that God raised him from the dead, you will be saved. For it is with your heart that you believe and are justified, and it is with your mouth that you confess and are saved (Romans 10:9-10, *NIV*).

Scriptures to Memorize

Passage   **Target Memorization Date**

Month _____

Monday	Tuesday	Wednesday	Thursday	Friday	Saturday	Sunday
Date __/__/__	Date __/__/__	Date __/__/__	Date __/__/__	Date __/__/__	Date __/__/__	Date __/__/__
Date __/__/__	Date __/__/__	Date __/__/__	Date __/__/__	Date __/__/__	Date __/__/__	Date __/__/__
Date __/__/__	Date __/__/__	Date __/__/__	Date __/__/__	Date __/__/__	Date __/__/__	Date __/__/__
Date __/__/__	Date __/__/__	Date __/__/__	Date __/__/__	Date __/__/__	Date __/__/__	Date __/__/__
Date __/__/__	Date __/__/__	Date __/__/__	Date __/__/__	Date __/__/__	Date __/__/__	Date __/__/__

Calendar

/// 25 ///

Month_____

Monday	Tuesday	Wednesday	Thursday	Friday	Saturday	Sunday
Date __/__/__	Date __/__/__	Date __/__/__	Date __/__/__	Date __/__/__	Date __/__/__	Date __/__/__
Date __/__/__	Date __/__/__	Date __/__/__	Date __/__/__	Date __/__/__	Date __/__/__	Date __/__/__
Date __/__/__	Date __/__/__	Date __/__/__	Date __/__/__	Date __/__/__	Date __/__/__	Date __/__/__
Date __/__/__	Date __/__/__	Date __/__/__	Date __/__/__	Date __/__/__	Date __/__/__	Date __/__/__
Date __/__/__	Date __/__/__	Date __/__/__	Date __/__/__	Date __/__/__	Date __/__/__	Date __/__/__

www.PursueGod.com

Month_____

Monday	Tuesday	Wednesday	Thursday	Friday	Saturday	Sunday
Date ___/___/___	Date ___/___/___	Date ___/___/___	Date ___/___/___	Date ___/___/___	Date ___/___/___	Date ___/___/___
Date ___/___/___	Date ___/___/___	Date ___/___/___	Date ___/___/___	Date ___/___/___	Date ___/___/___	Date ___/___/___
Date ___/___/___	Date ___/___/___	Date ___/___/___	Date ___/___/___	Date ___/___/___	Date ___/___/___	Date ___/___/___
Date ___/___/___	Date ___/___/___	Date ___/___/___	Date ___/___/___	Date ___/___/___	Date ___/___/___	Date ___/___/___
Date ___/___/___	Date ___/___/___	Date ___/___/___	Date ___/___/___	Date ___/___/___	Date ___/___/___	Date ___/___/___

Month _____

Monday	Tuesday	Wednesday	Thursday	Friday	Saturday	Sunday
Date ___/___/___	Date ___/___/___	Date ___/___/___	Date ___/___/___	Date ___/___/___	Date ___/___/___	Date ___/___/___
Date ___/___/___	Date ___/___/___	Date ___/___/___	Date ___/___/___	Date ___/___/___	Date ___/___/___	Date ___/___/___
Date ___/___/___	Date ___/___/___	Date ___/___/___	Date ___/___/___	Date ___/___/___	Date ___/___/___	Date ___/___/___
Date ___/___/___	Date ___/___/___	Date ___/___/___	Date ___/___/___	Date ___/___/___	Date ___/___/___	Date ___/___/___
Date ___/___/___	Date ___/___/___	Date ___/___/___	Date ___/___/___	Date ___/___/___	Date ___/___/___	Date ___/___/___

Calendar

Month_____

Monday	Tuesday	Wednesday	Thursday	Friday	Saturday	Sunday
Date ___/___/___	Date ___/___/___	Date ___/___/___	Date ___/___/___	Date ___/___/___	Date ___/___/___	Date ___/___/___
Date ___/___/___	Date ___/___/___	Date ___/___/___	Date ___/___/___	Date ___/___/___	Date ___/___/___	Date ___/___/___
Date ___/___/___	Date ___/___/___	Date ___/___/___	Date ___/___/___	Date ___/___/___	Date ___/___/___	Date ___/___/___
Date ___/___/___	Date ___/___/___	Date ___/___/___	Date ___/___/___	Date ___/___/___	Date ___/___/___	Date ___/___/___
Date ___/___/___	Date ___/___/___	Date ___/___/___	Date ___/___/___	Date ___/___/___	Date ___/___/___	Date ___/___/___

Calendar

Month _____

Monday	Tuesday	Wednesday	Thursday	Friday	Saturday	Sunday
Date ___/___/___	Date ___/___/___	Date ___/___/___	Date ___/___/___	Date ___/___/___	Date ___/___/___	Date ___/___/___
Date ___/___/___	Date ___/___/___	Date ___/___/___	Date ___/___/___	Date ___/___/___	Date ___/___/___	Date ___/___/___
Date ___/___/___	Date ___/___/___	Date ___/___/___	Date ___/___/___	Date ___/___/___	Date ___/___/___	Date ___/___/___
Date ___/___/___	Date ___/___/___	Date ___/___/___	Date ___/___/___	Date ___/___/___	Date ___/___/___	Date ___/___/___
Date ___/___/___	Date ___/___/___	Date ___/___/___	Date ___/___/___	Date ___/___/___	Date ___/___/___	Date ___/___/___

Calendar

www.PursueGod.com

Month_____

Monday	Tuesday	Wednesday	Thursday	Friday	Saturday	Sunday
Date ___/___/___	Date ___/___/___	Date ___/___/___	Date ___/___/___	Date ___/___/___	Date ___/___/___	Date ___/___/___
Date ___/___/___	Date ___/___/___	Date ___/___/___	Date ___/___/___	Date ___/___/___	Date ___/___/___	Date ___/___/___
Date ___/___/___	Date ___/___/___	Date ___/___/___	Date ___/___/___	Date ___/___/___	Date ___/___/___	Date ___/___/___
Date ___/___/___	Date ___/___/___	Date ___/___/___	Date ___/___/___	Date ___/___/___	Date ___/___/___	Date ___/___/___
Date ___/___/___	Date ___/___/___	Date ___/___/___	Date ___/___/___	Date ___/___/___	Date ___/___/___	Date ___/___/___

Calendar

Month_____

Monday	Tuesday	Wednesday	Thursday	Friday	Saturday	Sunday
Date __/__/__	Date __/__/__	Date __/__/__	Date __/__/__	Date __/__/__	Date __/__/__	Date __/__/__
Date __/__/__	Date __/__/__	Date __/__/__	Date __/__/__	Date __/__/__	Date __/__/__	Date __/__/__
Date __/__/__	Date __/__/__	Date __/__/__	Date __/__/__	Date __/__/__	Date __/__/__	Date __/__/__
Date __/__/__	Date __/__/__	Date __/__/__	Date __/__/__	Date __/__/__	Date __/__/__	Date __/__/__
Date __/__/__	Date __/__/__	Date __/__/__	Date __/__/__	Date __/__/__	Date __/__/__	Date __/__/__

Calendar

www.PursueGod.com

*Month*_____

Monday	Tuesday	Wednesday	Thursday	Friday	Saturday	Sunday
Date ___/___/___	Date ___/___/___	Date ___/___/___	Date ___/___/___	Date ___/___/___	Date ___/___/___	Date ___/___/___
Date ___/___/___	Date ___/___/___	Date ___/___/___	Date ___/___/___	Date ___/___/___	Date ___/___/___	Date ___/___/___
Date ___/___/___	Date ___/___/___	Date ___/___/___	Date ___/___/___	Date ___/___/___	Date ___/___/___	Date ___/___/___
Date ___/___/___	Date ___/___/___	Date ___/___/___	Date ___/___/___	Date ___/___/___	Date ___/___/___	Date ___/___/___
Date ___/___/___	Date ___/___/___	Date ___/___/___	Date ___/___/___	Date ___/___/___	Date ___/___/___	Date ___/___/___

*Month*_____

Monday	Tuesday	Wednesday	Thursday	Friday	Saturday	Sunday
Date __/__/__	Date __/__/__	Date __/__/__	Date __/__/__	Date __/__/__	Date __/__/__	Date __/__/__
Date __/__/__	Date __/__/__	Date __/__/__	Date __/__/__	Date __/__/__	Date __/__/__	Date __/__/__
Date __/__/__	Date __/__/__	Date __/__/__	Date __/__/__	Date __/__/__	Date __/__/__	Date __/__/__
Date __/__/__	Date __/__/__	Date __/__/__	Date __/__/__	Date __/__/__	Date __/__/__	Date __/__/__
Date __/__/__	Date __/__/__	Date __/__/__	Date __/__/__	Date __/__/__	Date __/__/__	Date __/__/__

Month_____

Monday	Tuesday	Wednesday	Thursday	Friday	Saturday	Sunday
Date ___/___/___	Date ___/___/___	Date ___/___/___	Date ___/___/___	Date ___/___/___	Date ___/___/___	Date ___/___/___
Date ___/___/___	Date ___/___/___	Date ___/___/___	Date ___/___/___	Date ___/___/___	Date ___/___/___	Date ___/___/___
Date ___/___/___	Date ___/___/___	Date ___/___/___	Date ___/___/___	Date ___/___/___	Date ___/___/___	Date ___/___/___
Date ___/___/___	Date ___/___/___	Date ___/___/___	Date ___/___/___	Date ___/___/___	Date ___/___/___	Date ___/___/___
Date ___/___/___	Date ___/___/___	Date ___/___/___	Date ___/___/___	Date ___/___/___	Date ___/___/___	Date ___/___/___

Calendar

www.PursueGod.com

Month_____

Monday	Tuesday	Wednesday	Thursday	Friday	Saturday	Sunday
Date ___/___/___	Date ___/___/___	Date ___/___/___	Date ___/___/___	Date ___/___/___	Date ___/___/___	Date ___/___/___
Date ___/___/___	Date ___/___/___	Date ___/___/___	Date ___/___/___	Date ___/___/___	Date ___/___/___	Date ___/___/___
Date ___/___/___	Date ___/___/___	Date ___/___/___	Date ___/___/___	Date ___/___/___	Date ___/___/___	Date ___/___/___
Date ___/___/___	Date ___/___/___	Date ___/___/___	Date ___/___/___	Date ___/___/___	Date ___/___/___	Date ___/___/___
Date ___/___/___	Date ___/___/___	Date ___/___/___	Date ___/___/___	Date ___/___/___	Date ___/___/___	Date ___/___/___

Calendar

www.PursueGod.com

Response

❋ I AM A NEW CREATION IN CHRIST!

Therefore, if anyone is in Christ, he is a new creation;
the old has gone, the new has come!
2 Corinthians 5:17, *NIV*

www.PursueGod.com

Response

Response

✱ I AM CALLED TO PREACH THE GOSPEL!

Go into all the world and preach the Good News to everyone, everywhere.
Mark 16:15, *NLT*

www.PursueGod.com

Response

---

* **I HAVE A GREAT FUTURE!**

  "For I know the plans I have for you," declares the LORD, "plans to prosper you and not to harm you, plans to give you hope and a future."

  Jeremiah 29:11, *NIV*

Response

❋ I CAN DO ALL THINGS THROUGH CHRIST!

I can do all things through Christ who strengthens me.
Philippians 4:13, *NKJV*

Response

Response

✳ BY HIS STRIPES I AM HEALED!

But he was wounded and crushed for our sins. He was beaten that we might have peace. He was whipped, and we were healed!
Isaiah 53:5, *NLT*

Response

NO WEAPON FORMED AGAINST ME SHALL PROSPER!

No weapon that is formed against you will prosper.

Isaiah 54:17, *NASB*

Response

_____

_____

_____

_____

_____

_____

_____

_____

_____

_____

_____

_____

_____

_____

_____

_____

_____

_____

_____

_____

_____

_____

_____

_____

_____

_____

_____

_____

_____

_____

_____

 I WILL NOT GIVE IN TO TEMPTATION!

*But remember that the temptations that come into your life are no different
from what others experience. And God is faithful. He will keep the temptation
from becoming so strong that you can't stand up against it. When you are tempted,
he will show you a way out so that you will not give in to it.*

1 Corinthians 10:13, *NLT*

Response

www.PursueGod.com

Response

✱ GOD WILL SPEAK TO ME TODAY AS I PRAY!

Call to me and I will answer you and tell you great and unsearchable things you do not know.

Jeremiah 33:3, *NIV*

Response

 I AM FREE IN CHRIST!

*It is for freedom that Christ has set us free. Stand firm, then,
and do not let yourselves be burdened again by a yoke of slavery.*

Galatians 5:1, *NIV*

Response

✳ I AM PURE IN CHRIST!

If we confess our sins, he is faithful and just and will forgive us our sins and purify us from all unrighteousness.

1 John 1:9, *NIV*

www.PursueGod.com

Response

Response

❋ I AM A NEW CREATION IN CHRIST!

*Therefore, if anyone is in Christ, he is a new creation;
the old has gone, the new has come!*

2 Corinthians 5:17, *NIV*

Response

_____

_____

_____

_____

_____

_____

_____

_____

_____

_____

_____

_____

_____

_____

_____

_____

_____

_____

_____

_____

_____

_____

_____

_____

_____

_____

_____

_____

_____

_____

_____

_____

✳ I AM CALLED TO PREACH THE GOSPEL!

Go into all the world and preach the Good News to everyone, everywhere.
Mark 16:15, *NLT*

Response

_____

✳ I HAVE A GREAT FUTURE!

*"For I know the plans I have for you," declares the LORD, "plans to prosper you
and not to harm you, plans to give you hope and a future."*

Jeremiah 29:11, *NIV*

Response

Response

✳ **I CAN DO ALL THINGS THROUGH CHRIST!**

I can do all things through Christ who strengthens me.
Philippians 4:13, *NKJV*

Response

_____

_____

_____

_____

_____

_____

_____

_____

_____

_____

_____

_____

_____

_____

_____

_____

_____

_____

_____

_____

_____

_____

_____

_____

_____

_____

_____

_____

_____

✳ BY HIS STRIPES I AM HEALED!

But he was wounded and crushed for our sins. He was beaten that
we might have peace. He was whipped, and we were healed!

Isaiah 53:5, *NLT*

Response

Response

 NO WEAPON FORMED AGAINST ME SHALL PROSPER!

No weapon that is formed against you will prosper.
Isaiah 54:17, *NASB*

Response

✳ I WILL NOT GIVE IN TO TEMPTATION!

But remember that the temptations that come into your life are no different from what others experience. And God is faithful. He will keep the temptation from becoming so strong that you can't stand up against it. When you are tempted, he will show you a way out so that you will not give in to it.

1 Corinthians 10:13, *NLT*

Response

Response

GOD WILL SPEAK TO ME TODAY AS I PRAY!

Call to me and I will answer you and tell you great and unsearchable things you do not know.

Jeremiah 33:3, *NIV*

Response

I AM FREE IN CHRIST!

It is for freedom that Christ has set us free. Stand firm, then, and do not let yourselves be burdened again by a yoke of slavery.

Galatians 5:1, *NIV*

Response

Response

 I AM PURE IN CHRIST!

*If we confess our sins, he is faithful and just and will forgive us
our sins and purify us from all unrighteousness.*

1 John 1:9, *NIV*

Response

_____
_____
_____
_____
_____
_____
_____
_____
_____
_____
_____
_____
_____
_____
_____
_____
_____
_____
_____
_____
_____
_____
_____
_____
_____
_____
_____
_____
_____
_____
_____
_____

 I AM A NEW CREATION IN CHRIST!

Therefore, if anyone is in Christ, he is a new creation;
the old has gone, the new has come!
2 Corinthians 5:17, _NIV_

Response

Response

✳ **I AM CALLED TO PREACH THE GOSPEL!**

Go into all the world and preach the Good News to everyone, everywhere.
Mark 16:15, *NLT*

Response

I HAVE A GREAT FUTURE!

"For I know the plans I have for you," declares the LORD, "plans to prosper you and not to harm you, plans to give you hope and a future."
Jeremiah 29:11, *NIV*

Response

Response

✳ I CAN DO ALL THINGS THROUGH CHRIST!

I can do all things through Christ who strengthens me.
Philippians 4:13, *NKJV*

Response

Response

✴ BY HIS STRIPES I AM HEALED!

But he was wounded and crushed for our sins. He was beaten that we might have peace. He was whipped, and we were healed!

Isaiah 53:5, *NLT*

Response

Response

_____

_____

_____

_____

_____

_____

_____

_____

_____

_____

_____

_____

_____

_____

_____

_____

_____

_____

_____

_____

_____

_____

_____

_____

_____

_____

_____

_____

_____

✱ NO WEAPON FORMED AGAINST ME SHALL PROSPER!

No weapon that is formed against you will prosper.
Isaiah 54:17, _NASB_

Response

Response

 I WILL NOT GIVE IN TO TEMPTATION!

But remember that the temptations that come into your life are no different from what others experience. And God is faithful. He will keep the temptation from becoming so strong that you can't stand up against it. When you are tempted, he will show you a way out so that you will not give in to it.

1 Corinthians 10:13, *NLT*

Response

Response

GOD WILL SPEAK TO ME TODAY AS I PRAY!

*Call to me and I will answer you and tell you great and
unsearchable things you do not know.*

Jeremiah 33:3, *NIV*

Response

✳ I AM FREE IN CHRIST!

*It is for freedom that Christ has set us free. Stand firm, then,
and do not let yourselves be burdened again by a yoke of slavery.*
Galatians 5:1, *NIV*

Response

Response

I AM PURE IN CHRIST!

*If we confess our sins, he is faithful and just and will forgive us
our sins and purify us from all unrighteousness.*
1 John 1:9, *NIV*

Response

I AM A NEW CREATION IN CHRIST!

Therefore, if anyone is in Christ, he is a new creation;
the old has gone, the new has come!

2 Corinthians 5:17, *NIV*

Response

✳ I AM CALLED TO PREACH THE GOSPEL!

Go into all the world and preach the Good News to everyone, everywhere.
Mark 16:15, *NLT*

Response

_____
_____
_____
_____
_____
_____
_____
_____
_____
_____
_____
_____
_____
_____
_____
_____
_____
_____
_____
_____
_____
_____
_____
_____
_____
_____

✳ I HAVE A GREAT FUTURE!

"For I know the plans I have for you," declares the LORD, "plans to prosper you and not to harm you, plans to give you hope and a future."

Jeremiah 29:11, *NIV*

Response

Response

✱ I CAN DO ALL THINGS THROUGH CHRIST!

I can do all things through Christ who strengthens me.
Philippians 4:13, *NKJV*

Response

BY HIS STRIPES I AM HEALED!

But he was wounded and crushed for our sins. He was beaten that we might have peace. He was whipped, and we were healed!
Isaiah 53:5, *NLT*

Response

Response

NO WEAPON FORMED AGAINST ME SHALL PROSPER!

No weapon that is formed against you will prosper.
Isaiah 54:17, *NASB*

www.PursueGod.com

Response

_____

_____

_____

_____

_____

_____

_____

_____

_____

_____

_____

_____

_____

_____

_____

_____

_____

_____

_____

_____

_____

_____

_____

_____

_____

_____

_____

_____

✳ I WILL NOT GIVE IN TO TEMPTATION!

But remember that the temptations that come into your life are no different from what others experience. And God is faithful. He will keep the temptation from becoming so strong that you can't stand up against it. When you are tempted, he will show you a way out so that you will not give in to it.

1 Corinthians 10:13, *NLT*

Response

Response

GOD WILL SPEAK TO ME TODAY AS I PRAY!

Call to me and I will answer you and tell you great and unsearchable things you do not know.

Jeremiah 33:3, *NIV*

Response

✳ I AM FREE IN CHRIST!

It is for freedom that Christ has set us free. Stand firm, then, and do not let yourselves be burdened again by a yoke of slavery.

Galatians 5:1, *NIV*

Response

✱ I AM PURE IN CHRIST!

*If we confess our sins, he is faithful and just and will forgive us
our sins and purify us from all unrighteousness.*

1 John 1:9, *NIV*

Response

Response

✳ I AM A NEW CREATION IN CHRIST!

*Therefore, if anyone is in Christ, he is a new creation;
the old has gone, the new has come!*

2 Corinthians 5:17, *NIV*

www.PursueGod.com

Response

Response

I AM CALLED TO PREACH THE GOSPEL!

Go into all the world and preach the Good News to everyone, everywhere.
Mark 16:15, *NLT*

Response

_____
_____
_____
_____
_____
_____
_____
_____
_____
_____
_____
_____
_____
_____
_____
_____
_____
_____
_____
_____
_____
_____
_____
_____
_____
_____
_____
_____
_____

✳ I HAVE A GREAT FUTURE!

*"For I know the plans I have for you," declares the LORD, "plans to prosper you
and not to harm you, plans to give you hope and a future."*
Jeremiah 29:11, *NIV*

www.PursueGod.com

Response

Response

* **I CAN DO ALL THINGS THROUGH CHRIST!**

I can do all things through Christ who strengthens me.
Philippians 4:13, *NKJV*

Response

_____

_____

_____

_____

_____

_____

_____

_____

_____

_____

_____

_____

_____

_____

_____

_____

_____

_____

_____

_____

_____

_____

_____

_____

_____

_____

 BY HIS STRIPES I AM HEALED!

But he was wounded and crushed for our sins. He was beaten that we might have peace. He was whipped, and we were healed!
Isaiah 53:5, *NLT*

Response

www.PursueGod.com

Response

 NO WEAPON FORMED AGAINST ME SHALL PROSPER!

No weapon that is formed against you will prosper.

Isaiah 54:17, *NASB*

www.PursueGod.com

Response

_____

_____

_____

_____

_____

_____

_____

_____

_____

_____

_____

_____

_____

_____

_____

_____

_____

_____

_____

_____

_____

_____

_____

_____

_____

_____

_____

_____

_____

_____

_____

_____

_____

_____

_____

✳ **I WILL NOT GIVE IN TO TEMPTATION!**

*But remember that the temptations that come into your life are no different
from what others experience. And God is faithful. He will keep the temptation
from becoming so strong that you can't stand up against it. When you are tempted,
he will show you a way out so that you will not give in to it.*

1 Corinthians 10:13, *NLT*

Response

www.PursueGod.com

Response

GOD WILL SPEAK TO ME TODAY AS I PRAY!

Call to me and I will answer you and tell you great and unsearchable things you do not know.

Jeremiah 33:3, *NIV*

Response

Response

I AM FREE IN CHRIST!

It is for freedom that Christ has set us free. Stand firm, then, and do not let yourselves be burdened again by a yoke of slavery.
Galatians 5:1, *NIV*

Response

Response

❋ I AM PURE IN CHRIST!

*If we confess our sins, he is faithful and just and will forgive us
our sins and purify us from all unrighteousness.*
1 John 1:9, *NIV*

Response

Response

✳ I AM A NEW CREATION IN CHRIST!

Therefore, if anyone is in Christ, he is a new creation;
the old has gone, the new has come!

2 Corinthians 5:17, *NIV*

www.PursueGod.com

Response

Journal Pages

Response

✳ **I AM CALLED TO PREACH THE GOSPEL!**

Go into all the world and preach the Good News to everyone, everywhere.
Mark 16:15, *NLT*

Response

_____

✱ I HAVE A GREAT FUTURE!

"For I know the plans I have for you," declares the LORD, "plans to prosper you and not to harm you, plans to give you hope and a future."
Jeremiah 29:11, *NIV*

Response

I CAN DO ALL THINGS THROUGH CHRIST!

I can do all things through Christ who strengthens me.
Philippians 4:13, *NKJV*

Response

Response

 BY HIS STRIPES I AM HEALED!

But he was wounded and crushed for our sins. He was beaten that we might have peace. He was whipped, and we were healed!
Isaiah 53:5, *NLT*

Response

Response

✳ NO WEAPON FORMED AGAINST ME SHALL PROSPER!

No weapon that is formed against you will prosper.
Isaiah 54:17, *NASB*

Response

———————————————
———————————————
———————————————
———————————————

❋ I WILL NOT GIVE IN TO TEMPTATION!

But remember that the temptations that come into your life are no different from what others experience. And God is faithful. He will keep the temptation from becoming so strong that you can't stand up against it. When you are tempted, he will show you a way out so that you will not give in to it.

1 Corinthians 10:13, *NLT*

Response

Response

GOD WILL SPEAK TO ME TODAY AS I PRAY!

Call to me and I will answer you and tell you great and unsearchable things you do not know.

Jeremiah 33:3, *NIV*

Response

I AM FREE IN CHRIST!

It is for freedom that Christ has set us free. Stand firm, then,
and do not let yourselves be burdened again by a yoke of slavery.
Galatians 5:1, *NIV*

Response

www.PursueGod.com

Response

I AM PURE IN CHRIST!

If we confess our sins, he is faithful and just and will forgive us our sins and purify us from all unrighteousness.

1 John 1:9, *NIV*

Response

Response

(blank ruled journal lines)

✳ I AM A NEW CREATION IN CHRIST!

Therefore, if anyone is in Christ, he is a new creation; the old has gone, the new has come!

2 Corinthians 5:17, *NIV*

Response

www.PursueGod.com

Recommended Materials

The Attitude of Faith
By Pastor Frank Damazio

The "yes" attitude is the biblical attitude for living life. God's Word is faithful, and His message is absolute, certain and guaranteed. God does not vacillate in His message or His plans, and neither should we. More than just positive thinking or mind over matter, author Frank Damazio describes an attitude established upon the Word of God. More than fantasizing or imagining whatever we want, it is saying yes to the God who can and will do exceedingly and abundantly above all that we ask or think. For more resources from Pastor Frank Damazio, go to www.FrankDamazio.com.

What Now
By Pastor Marc Estes

God's intent is that we live life purposefully and deliberately, not randomly. Each of us has been given a measure of passions, gifts, talents and abilities to invest during our lifetime. How we use or misuse them creates consequences. Ultimately, each of us will be held responsible for what we were given and whether we were faithful in making our lives count. *What Now* will help you to make sense of who you are and where you are going! What makes this book unique are seven distinct self-discovery tests that will specifically define key areas of your life. This is a must-read. For more resources from Pastor Marc Estes, go to www.MarcEstes.com.

Generation Unleashed® // Saving Power CD/DVD

The Generation Unleashed band firmly believes that the presence of God changes people's lives. This CD captures this generation's passion and desire to see God lifted high with songs that create a culture of presence-driven worship. The Generation Unleashed band takes God's message of hope and freedom in Jesus Christ to churches, conferences, cities and nations worldwide. To find out more, go to www.Facebook.com/GenerationUnleashed.

Portland Bible College

Portland Bible College

For more than 40 years, the passion of Portland Bible College has been to partner with the Church to develop leaders in all areas of life that will influence, impact and transform their world. Portland Bible College offers training in pastoral leadership, worship and creative arts, pastoral counseling and youth ministry, along with a humanities program designed for university transfer. At Portland Bible College, you'll find a vibrant campus where you will experience God's presence, clearly understand His Word, walk with a team of staff and pastors committed to your success, and be equipped to fulfill God's vision for your life! For more information, go to www.PortlandBibleCollege.com.

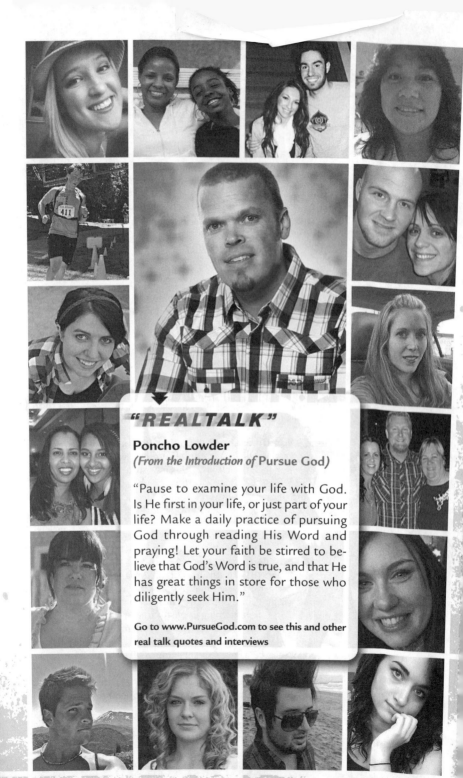

"REALTALK"

Poncho Lowder
(From the Introduction of Pursue God)

"Pause to examine your life with God. Is He first in your life, or just part of your life? Make a daily practice of pursuing God through reading His Word and praying! Let your faith be stirred to believe that God's Word is true, and that He has great things in store for those who diligently seek Him."

Go to www.PursueGod.com to see this and other real talk quotes and interviews